W9-AZV-059

all about ferrets

MERVIN F. ROBERTS

Distributed in the U.S.A. by T.F.H. Publications, Inc., 211 West Sylvania Avenue, P.O. Box 27, Neptune City, N.J. 07753; in England by T.F.H. (Gt. Britain) Ltd., 13 Nutley Lane, Reigate, Surrey; in Canada to the book store and library trade by Clarke, Irwin & Company, Clarwin House, 791 St. Clair Avenue West, Toronto 10, Ontario; in Canada to the pet trade by Rolf C. Hagen Ltd., 3225 Sartelon Street, Montreal 382, Quebec; in Southeast Asia by Y.W. Ong, 9 Lorong 36 Geylang, Singapore 14; in Australia and the south Pacific by Pet Imports Pty. Ltd., P.O. Box 149, Brookvale 2100, N.S.W., Australia.

Cover photo by Jeremy Dodd.

Photography:
   Jeremy Dodd: 1, 4, 5, 8, 14, 16, 19, 20, 22, 29, 30,
             31, 32, 35, 39, 41, 47
   John Dommers: 9, 12, 13, 17, 21, 24, 25, 28

ISBN 0-87666-914-3

© **1977 by T.F.H. Publications, Inc. Ltd.**

Contents

Introduction

All right, I give up—what is it?

Today, not many people recognize a ferret when they see one, but as a matter of fact, these wonderful pets have been domesticated since Biblical times. Until recently, most of them have been kept in cages, but lately ferrets have become popular as house pets. For an introduction, let's meet the ferret and learn his names. When an animal has been closely associated with man for a long time, it accumulates names. The closer and longer the association, the greater the number of names.

The author with one of his favorite ferret pets.

The two colors most commonly encountered among pet ferrets are
albino (above) and brown, also called sable.

Also, animals' names are applied to humans who display the animals' traits, like mousy or owlish or catty.

All this is true of the ferret. Over the past few centuries, the English spelling has varied: fyrette, forferet, firret, ferrit. The word seems to stem from the late Latin *furon-em*, which also gave us the Italian *furone* = robber. Today our dictionaries make ferret useful as a noun (a narrow tape or ribbon) and as a verb (to extract from a lurking place, to search out with keenness, to draw out by shrewd questioning). The word shrewd itself, of course, is derived from the shrew—a tiny, perverse, evil, artful, wily, cunning animal not related to ferrets.

Female ferrets are called jills, bitches or does; males are hobs, dogs or bucks. The young are called kits.

Scientifically, our domestic ferret is usually now known as *Mustela putorius* and is of European and/or North African origin. This animal is so thoroughly domesticated that if one escapes in the U.S.A. he will surely die of exposure or starvation before establishing a wild population. There have been ferrets in the U.S. since soon after the first Englishmen arrived in New England, but even after 300 years of escaping or getting lost, there are still no established resident colonies of wild *M. putorius*.

However, we do have a native endangered species which is similar. This is the black-footed ferret, *Mustela nigripes* of our Great Plains area, but at the time of this writing it may already be extinct. The black-footed ferret is listed in the Red Book of Endangered Species. Its diet is mostly prairie dogs, and since prairie dogs have been severely reduced in numbers, the native wild ferret is probably doomed. But, regardless, our native ferret and your pet are **not** the same species.

It is customary in books like this to lay out the

branches of the tree of life, and right here is a good place to do it.

Kingdom—Animalia—Life, plants and fungi excluded

Phylum—Chordata—with a spinal cord

Subphylum—Vertebrata—with a backbone

Class—Mammalia—nurse their young

Subclass—Eutheria—with a placenta, excluding marsupials

Order—Carnivora—flesh-eaters

Suborder—Fissipeda—with separate toes, excluding seals and walruses

Family—Mustelidae—those who carry off mice

Genus—*Mustela*—ferrets and their ilk

Subgenus—*Putorius*—European polecats, from the Latin *putor* = stench

Species—*putorius*—the domestic ferret

Species—*furo*—an erroneous specific name for ferrets; forget it.

Authorities today agree that we should call our domestic ferret *Mustela putorius*, but we also know that it will breed freely with the wild European polecat and that this union produces fertile young which resemble both parents. So our ferret is really a domesticated polecat with its own name.

Other references to our pet call it *Mustela furo* or *Mustela putorius furo*, and still others suggest that it is the product of a cross between a wild European polecat and a wild European or Asiatic ferret. This latter animal, interestingly, doesn't seem to exist in zoos, museums, books, or even in the woods, so we might well discard that theory for the present.

In this book we will assume that all domestic ferrets are decendants of the European polecat, *Mustela putorius*, so we are pleased to call it by that scientific name. The dictionary tells us that *putorius* is derived from the

Alert, inquisitive and intelligent, the ferret has the capacity to become an excellent pet if it is treated with consideration and common sense.

It is best not to handle your ferret with undue familiarity until you and he have become friends and are used to one another—and one way to become friends with your ferret is to offer the animal an occasional treat in the form of an especially desirable tidbit.

Latin *putor*—a stench. It is unfortunate that our ferret has to bear the same disagreeably descriptive specific epithet as its wild forebear, because even though the name is aptly applied to polecats, it does not apply to ferrets. Actually the domestic ferret is not an especially smelly animal; with clean bedding, bathing and some procedures you can follow, your pet can be virtually odorless.

The classic example of an English ferret in Queen Victoria's time was a white or yellowish pink-eyed albino derived from 100% domesticated stock mated, reproduced and reared in captivity. This is an animal referred to as a pure-blooded ferret. Its scientific name then was *Mustelo furo.* However, in the British Isles and in much of northern Europe, a wild polecat was to be found. This polecat was known as the fitchew, foul marten, fitchet and foumart. It was a brown, dark-eyed and smelly animal. From time to time, ferret keepers would trap a wild male polecat and mate it to one of their domestic albino ferrets. The offspring made good hunters which were frequently more vigorous than purebred ferrets. The first generation of young were invariably colored dark, but by selective inbreeding the albino strain could later be sorted out genetically. Since ferrets are mature by eleven months, a few generations of controlled breeding by a fancier are no more time consuming than what is done by poultry, dog and cat breeders all the time.

Obviously, the European wild polecat and the domesticated white or yellow albinistic European ferret are, in fact, the same species. When mated, they produce fertile young which resemble their parents, and that, superficially but technically, is what "species" is all about.

Getting back to the European polecat for a moment, it might be worth mentioning that if a wild polecat mates in captivity with a domesticated ferret, the young are simply domestic ferrets. The major difference seems to be that the wild European polecat has but one litter per year, but the female ferret (and the domestic ferret/wild polecat cross) can produce two litters every year for as many as ten or fifteen years.

Much of this explanation is merely a clarification of facts which were all spelled out in the classic of 1897 titled *Ferrets* by Nicholas Everitt, published in London by Adam and Charles Black. Unfortunately, the author did not understand taxonomy or genetics well enough to make a valid conclusion, but his evidence, if you believe him, speaks for itself. So, then, there is but one species encompassing both the aforementioned varieties. The only significant technical differences seem to be that the wild ones are smellier, more vigorous and less tractable, and that they produce but one litter per year. So we have one domestic race (ferret) and one wild race (polecat) of the same species.

One nearly last word about names regards a man named Camel who was the proprietor of a business making artists' paint brushes, which he trademarked and sold as "Camels Hair Brushes," and the hair he used came from a musteline animal, perhaps a ferret, mink or sable. (The hair of a camel is wooly and useless for an artist's paint brush.) Still another brush used in France for painting of glaze colors on ceramic ware is called a *putois*, and it is said to be made from ferret or polecat hair.

Finally, the nearest relative of the native American black-footed ferret is probably the Siberian polecat, *Mustela eversmanni*. It is easy to speculate that a migration took place during the time when there was a land bridge between Alaska and Siberia, but there is no hard evidence to absolutely prove the speculation.

Ferrets respond well to affection, and some derive great satisfaction from being stroked and fondled once they have become hand-tame.

There are no differences in temperament—or any other significant factor regarding the ferret's capacity to be a good pet—between the different color varieties available. Obviously the sable ferret shown above with the author and the albino shown opposite with its young friend both are able to respond to affection and good care.

Handling

Your ferret will enjoy your company. He may chuckle as you tickle his belly. He will fall asleep in your arms. He will crawl all over you if he has a chance. He will curl up in your hat or your coat pocket.

When your new pet arrives, have a secure nest available for him to rest in. Remember to provide a spot with cat litter or paper where he can relieve himself. Offer him a meal, a generous meal, but with absolutely no more than an ounce of evaporated milk, and plenty of fresh raw hamburger meat. Plenty for a young ferret

When first becoming acquainted with your ferret you should use gloves in handling your pet. A ferret should be handled for the first time only after it has had a full meal.

would be two heaping tablespoons full. Let him rest if he was shaken up in transit. Only after your pet is rested and *full of food* should you pick him up for the first time.

Take him up by grasping firmly around his forelegs. Don't grab his skin or his middle or his neck or his tail—but simply bring your hand over his back from the rear and then wrap your thumb around his shoulder on one side and align the next two fingers over the back of his neck and the two remaining fingers around his other shoulder. Support his lower body with your other hand. Be firm but gentle and your pet will enjoy your attention.

Once you and your pet become accustomed to each other, you can take more liberties, but you should start "according to the book" to avoid mishaps.

Choosing a Ferret

If your local pet shop stocks ferrets or can get one or two for you, this is probably the best way to go; it is certainly easier to purchase your pet from a local retailer than to order one from a mail-order seller—and it might be cheaper too. Your pet dealer also can make sure that your pet has been inoculated for distemper, a wise precaution. If you cannot obtain a ferret through your pet shop, look through magazines that carry advertisements for pet animals not normally carried in petshops.

Note that adult male ferrets establish territories and will sometimes defend them vigorously. But don't try to remake your pet; rather enjoy it for what it is. If you are going to have more than one ferret, get yourself a pair or two or more females, but don't get more than one male.

The ferret is a lithe, sinuous animal well designed for twisting and turning and all-around acrobatics on (and below) the ground, but you can provide a much better playground than a bookrack for your pet(s) by constructing a maze arrangement from plastic pipe material.

Opposite:
The ferret's agility allows it to arrange its body in many different poses. Sometimes it adopts distinctly feline postures, but at other times it assumes positions that only a ferret or one of its close relatives in the weasel family could adopt.

Your pet will be tame when it comes to you or it will soon become tame if you treat it with firm, affectionate and thoughtful care, so it really doesn't matter whether you buy a juvenile (kit) or an adult.

Males are usually larger than females and more placid throughout the year. Some females tend to be a little nervous during the springtime breeding season. Some people think that males have a bit more odor than females, but regardless, most people will hardly notice it. Actually, ferret odor is usually milder than the smell of a $7,500 mink coat on a damp day.

You may wish to have your veterinarian castrate your young adult male ferret; this is done with many domestic animals including swine, sheep, horses, cattle, dogs and cats. A male ferret is castrated the same way as a male dog. A young adult female ferret, likewise, may be altered if you do not wish to breed her. Female ferrets are altered in the same manner as a female cat.

Color is meaningless in terms of disposition or longevity, size or any other trait. Choose the color which appeals most to you. Generally, a brown is the least expensive and a pink-eyed albino costs about five dollars more. The "new" colors—Siamese and silver—sometimes command an additional premium, but nothing is different except the color.

Most ferret fanciers at one time or another think that perhaps their brown pet is really the rare, endangered black-footed ferret, *Mustela nigripes*. No such luck. It is just a coincidence that the markings of the black-footed ferret superficially resemble those of your pet. One detail to watch for is the color of the tail, which is dark for only one-third of its length on the black-footed ferret but dark for more than one-half—and often the entire—length on the domesticated ferret. Also, your pet, by comparison, has coarser hair and longer guard hairs than its wild American cousin.

This is an adult female ferret. The vaginal opening is about an inch forward of the anus; when the ferret is in heat her vaginal opening will be somewhat larger and perhaps inflamed.

It is natural for a ferret to be skittish and apprehensive when it is first becoming accustomed to handling by human beings. Ferrets are individualistic enough to differ in their temperaments to a certain extent; some ferrets take readily to being handled and actually seem to like the experience, whereas others remain aloof to handling all their lives.

One way to relax a ferret somewhat during the process in which it is being trained not to resent handling is to offer it food treats.

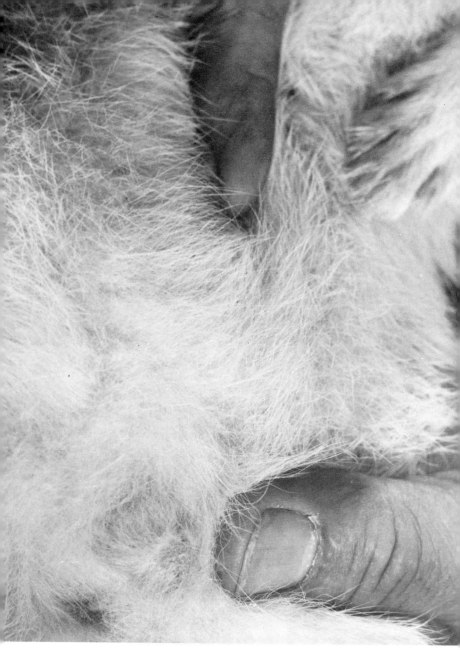

Closeup of the genital region of a young male albino ferret. The scrotum is in front of the thumb, near the anus, and the penis is nearly two inches forward of the other finger, mostly hidden by belly hair.

If you personally select a pet it should appear healthy, frisky, alert and dry at both ends. A wet tail, runny nose or dripping eyes is not a sign of abundant good health, and no novice should saddle himself with a problem at the start. The nose should be cool and damp —like a dog's.

By choosing a healthy specimen of any age and color and either sex (or no remaining sex at all), you will have a pet you will enjoy either in an outdoor cage or in the home. In many ways, ferrets make one think of tiny, short-legged, vivacious kittens ever ready to investigate anything and ever ready to roll over and be tickled.

Training and Taming

The best time to start taming your pet is right after he has had a filling meal. He will be relaxed, even lethargic, and you should pick him up then firmly and gently and cradle him in your arms. Go at this gradually. Be firm, but don't squeeze or pinch. *Pay strict attention to the ferret. You have a lot to learn.* For the first few encounters, work alone. Clear the area of other animals and people. Reduce the possibility of distracting influences.

For starters, hold him when *he* wants to be held and put him down when *he* "wants down." How will you know? When he licks you a few times. When he bites you gently before he bites you less gently. When he squirms. When his voice has an irritated edge to it.

Reach with your hand, not with a single pointed finger. A single pointed finger to a nearsighted ferret looks like a pink mouse. Pick up the ferret in a gloved hand with your shirtsleeves rolled down and the cuffs buttoned. Don't expect to be bitten, but do take some simple precautions, though they will probably be un-

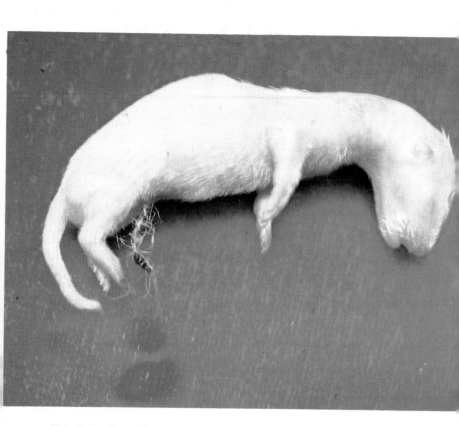

This baby ferret is two days old.

Opposite:
Above: A four-day-old ferret shown being weighed to determine rate of growth. *Below:* The same baby ferret shown in closeup in the scale pan to show relative size. Notice that the four-day-old ferret shown here does not look appreciably different from the two-day-old ferret shown opposite, apart from the slightly more opened eyes and the greater definition to the ear structure.

necessary. Obviously, if you purchased your ferret in a pet shop you will know how tame it is before bringing it home, but in new surroundings it would be a good idea to go at it with some caution anyway.

Meat on your fingers suggests meat to be bitten, but milk on your fingers suggests licking or lapping. So if your ferret is a little flighty or nervous, feed it a substantial meaty meal and wind up with a little bread soaked in undiluted evaporated milk. Not condensed milk, but evaporated milk. If some milk gets from your fingers to the ferret's mouth, you have come a long way toward taming a nippy newcomer. A little milk for a hungry ferret will only excite it, but a little milk for a nearly sated ferret will surely delight it.

Once your ferret shows some pleasure in being held or riding on your shoulder or in your coat pocket, you should not neglect it. Continue to hand feed, pet and even tickle your pet—if he enjoys being tickled—and most do.

Handle your pet at least once a day, after it has had a good meal. Some of his odor may rub off on your clothes; this will help in the taming process, since a ferret is not prone to bite something that smells like himself.

Signals

Your ferret is not a noisy animal. It will rattle its food tray as a gentle reminder to you from time to time. This is natural in a creature that stores little or no fat against lean days. If you are a little slow in attending to regular feedings of your pet—or skimpy with the food—your ferret might learn to get your attention by making some noise. Ferrets are not stupid.

In addition to food tray rattling, ferrets do chatter and chuckle and giggle and mumble. The noise a ferret makes is not loud, but it is certainly full of meaning. Your pet will talk to itself, to you and to other ferrets, if you have more than one.

If your pet is treated thoughtfully and gently all its life, you may never be reminded of the derivation of names like *putorius* and *foetedis*. If it is cornered or chased or shaken or otherwise abused, it may discharge some of its musk almost in the manner of a skunk. Assume that if this happens, it is because *you* did something wrong. Usually your pet is odorless or nearly so. Strong ferret odor is a signal that something is wrong.

Another emotionally triggered signal is the raising of its fur. An angry ferret will raise its fur (probably by adrenal gland action) until it looks twice as large as normal. Of course, cats also do it, and dogs raise the hair on their backs in similar manner.

Another emotional outburst of ferrets is biting. If your pet is squeezed or pinched whenever it is picked up, it will bite every time someone reaches for it. If it is fed a treat or cuddled or tickled a little, it will respond in like manner. It's as simple as that.

Housing

Your adult ferret will live alone or with its mate, or with its juvenile offspring, or several families will do all right together. Juveniles and, of course, juvenile littermates, are also o.k. together. You should separate females about to whelp and give them absolute privacy until the kits are at least three weeks old. Then the adult male may be joined with his family.

The physical structure of your ferret's living quarters depends on your climate and, of course, whether

By the time they have reached an age of sixteen days (the age at which they are shown in both photos here), these babies are at their most appealing. These baby ferrets, incidentally, are *not* albinos; the light color shown is normal for baby sables.

It is not easy—especially for beginning ferret-keepers—to distinguish between the sexes of ferrets without making an examination of the genital areas of the animals involved. The albino above is an adult male; the sable below is an adult female.

you are keeping a house pet or perhaps several outside pets.

Your animal is not much of a climber, so the outside cage need not be more than two feet high. He does require exercise, so a screened area two feet high and no less than 18 inches wide and perhaps three, or better still four, feet long would be adequate for one or two specimens. The ferret likes a small, warm, dry nest attached to its cage. An enclosed section measuring no less than two feet by two feet by 18 inches high is ample for two or three ferrets, or a jill with kits. The opening from the cage to the enclosure could well be a round hole four inches in diameter. A baffle plate in wintertime inside the doorway will stop some of the weather from getting in, and this will improve the quality of life for your pet tremendously.

This homemade ferret cage is sturdily constructed and is big enough to house a number of ferrets. The partially screened front allows ventilation in the free area, and the nest box is partitioned off separately. The roof slants to allow the rain to run off, and the legs of the cage provide a good clearance above the ground.

Victor Marquéz is amused by the chickens which always show up at ferret-feeding time—something is bound to slip through the floor grating, they hope. This view shows how the lid of the cage is supported at the rear.

If you intend to house your ferret in such an outdoor cage (a two-compartment rabbit hutch with a somewhat smaller door is a fair approximation) and your winters are really cold (like below zero Fahrenheit for several days at a time), you should own two ferrets so they can cuddle up and keep each other warm. They don't hibernate.

On mink ranches, ferrets are kept in mink cages, and the only concession to their possible warm-country origin is to double them up in wintertime.

The closed section of the hutch should be furnished with soft hay, and that's about it for the nest. The screened area needs a water supply or water dish and a food dish. Both should be easy to clean and difficult to tip over. The cage should be well off the ground—con-

This outdoor cage is completely portable and can be shifted around on the property to take advantage of climatic conditions. Here it has been situated under trees to provide shade.

THE WORLD'S LARGEST SELECTION OF PET AND ANIMAL BOOKS

T.F.H. Publications publishes more than 900 books covering many hobby aspects (dogs,

. . . BIRDS . .

. . CATS . . .

. . . ANIMALS . . .

. . . DOGS . .

cats, birds, fish, small animals, etc.), plus books dealing with more purely scientific aspects of the animal world (such as books about fossils, corals, sea shells, whales and octopuses). Whether you are a beginner or an advanced hobbyist you will find exactly what you're looking for among our complete listing of books. For a free catalog fill out the form on the other side of this page and mail it today. All T.F.H. books are recyclable.

. . FISH . . .

THE WORLD'S LARGEST SELECTION OF PET AND ANIMAL BOOKS

T.F.H. Publications publishes more than 900 books covering many hobby aspects (dogs,

. . CATS . . .

. . . BIRDS . .

. . . ANIMALS . . .

. . . DOGS . .

. . FISH . . .

cats, birds, fish, small animals, etc.), plus books dealing with more purely scientific aspects of the animal world (such as books about fossils, corals, sea shells, whales and octopuses). Whether you are a beginner or an advanced hobbyist you will find exactly what you're looking for among our complete listing of books. For a free catalog fill out the form on the other side of this page and mail it today. All T.F.H. books are recyclable.

stant dampness is a most serious threat to ferret health. The cage bottom should be open enough to permit urine and solid wastes to pass through or be flushed through with a hose. Since these animals are naturally clean and will almost always defecate in the same place—usually a corner away from where they sleep—you might provide a tray with cat litter in the place they choose. There are several techniques for handling their wastes, and you will quickly figure out the method that suits your pet and you best. To begin with, keep the cage simple and easy to clean.

If you plan to have a ferret free in your home, you have to be smart, adaptable and tolerant. No detailed advice is really necessary. Treat your new pet as you would a new kitten and you will find it clean, smart and resourceful.

When you arrange the housing of your pet ferret, you should try to create the longest path between food, soil tray and nest box. Use ingenuity and common sense. Feed water through an inverted drip bottle. You can purchase a good one at your pet shop. Although it looks simple enough for you to do yourself, it is surprising how difficult it is to assemble a bottle, a rubber stopper with a hole, and a bent tube that all fit each other. Remember that ferrets are inquisitive and active and playful; if you don't fasten the water bottle securely, they will soon have it down and rolling about the cage like a soccer ball.

The food dish might well be heavy metal with a broad base. An old cast iron saucepan or frying pan shape perhaps six or eight inches in diameter is ample. Rest assured, if your ferret can move it, he will. Situate it well away from the large, deep litter tray. Since ferrets tend to back into a corner, you should put the tray in a corner and perhaps fold paper over the edges to simplify clean-up. The litter could be a commercially prepared cat litter or your own calcined clay, vermiculite, beach sand, dry sawdust or woodchips. If you make the clean-up part of your petkeeping simple and easy for yourself, your enjoyment of your pet will increase manyfold.

Adjust yourself to the idea that you will not change your ferret's habits, but rather you should act with him according to *his* way of life. It is not at all difficult, but if you find it too much, the humane thing to do is to give the animal to someone who wants to provide the care it deserves.

If you do things right, feeding and cleaning will take only a few minutes a day, and your pet is available all its remaining waking hours to intrigue, entertain, educate and amuse you.

Escapes and Captures

After 2000 plus years of domestication, ferrets are now in a transition stage. It will not likely establish itself in the wild in the U.S.A., since its requirements for food and climate are too limiting and its competitors and enemies are already too well adjusted. You can get an argument about this, of course. Some people—including some people who are concerned with the formulation and administration of laws governing the release or escape of pet animals into the wild—feel that ferrets *can* establish themselves and become economically and ecologically destructive.

In any event, your pet needs you. The trouble is that he doesn't always remember that he needs you. He is an inveterate investigator, searcher, prober, poker and snoop. He is drawn into tunnels and holes like a compulsive gambler is drawn to the racetrack.

If he cannot find a satisfactory tunnel to explore, he will dig one and then spend hours exploring it. One

The nest box is about 18" by 24" by 20" high. It is really too large for one, two or even three ferrets, but it is useful if a litter of seven is to be raised with their jill. The 20" height is barely high enough to slow down the potential escapee visible at left.

oft-repeated refrain of old-time ferreters was that they lost a ferret in a hole and had to wait it out or come back hours later to recover the little hunter.

What generally happened was that the ferret found its prey—a rat or perhaps a rabbit—at the dead end of a tunnel, and killed it there. Had the tunnel been open at both ends, the prey would have exited as soon as he sensed the presence of his enemy. A ferret is not a killer out of habit but out of hunger. He will proceed to eat what he kills right on the spot. The only exception might be in the case of an adult with kits being weaned in the nest. Then, if possible, the jill will carry food back to her babies. So then here is the situation: a three-pound rabbit freshly killed in its tunnel five feet from the portal and a one-pound tired and hungry ferret beside it. The next two acts in the scenario are obvious. First to eat and second to sleep. Total elapsed time—two to nine hours.

No amount of sweet talk could help the old-time ferreter, and today ferrets still act just that way. So what do you do? Leave a small bowl (one or two ounces) of evaporated milk and a box with your ferret's own bedding nearby. There is an excellent chance that within ten hours you will find the milk gone and your ferret asleep in his box.

It might be a good idea to anticipate escapes. Build a box or two in advance for this nearly certain eventuality. The box need not have a sophisticated latching/trapping mechanism. Your ferret will likely be happy to remain inside his little bedroom whether or not the door latches. A box the size of a shoebox with a ferret-size hole in one end and some bedding from the animal's nestbox inside is all the "trap" you probably will need, but for a special case, try a humane live-trap like the famous Havahart. Bait it with a piece of chicken or raw beef liver and come back for your pet in a few hours, or sit it out.

If you wish to walk your pet on a leash, you must first harness it. A neck collar will not work. Since a ferret's head is hardly wider than its neck, a collar will choke the animal before it can be made small enough to remain always behind the skull. The harness which will work is the figure-eight harness designed for cats; these harnesses are available in pet shops. Choose a small one. One loop will cross the chest and the second loop will pass under the ribs just behind the forelegs. A snug harness will work, but really, ferrets were just not made for this sort of thing.

Cleanliness

Although several of the items in this chapter have been mentioned elsewhere, it is appropriate to assemble them in one place under one heading. To begin with, your pet ferret doesn't want to be dirty. The proof is easy for you to establish. Provide a ferret with the conveniences to keep clean and it will. Immaculately clean and only slightly musky—even a male. Let's consider ferret habits one by one and then design a home and a lifestyle to suit these habits.

Ferrets prefer to relieve themselves when backed into a corner. You should provide a *deep* litter box made of metal or plastic which is easy for you to empty but impossible for your pet to overturn or dig out. An ideal size for an adult or a few juveniles would be about 10 x 15 x 4 inches deep. Place no more than one inch and a half of litter in the box. Pile it high in the corners, because that's where the action is. Sawdust, wood chips, sandy earth or prepared litter you can purchase in your pet shop will do nicely. Just be sure that the litter is in no way similar to the bedding you provide. No sense confusing the little fellow.

The size of the nest box is also something to think about. The ancestor of our ferret likely slept in an abandoned rabbit warren. It was not especially commodious, and it was never used as a toilet. A ferret doesn't want to sleep in or even very near his own mess. Keep the nest box small. A pair of ferrets will do nicely in a hay-filled box a foot by fifteen inches by a foot or more high. The height should be at least one foot for your convenience in handling the animals. A shallow box makes for easy escapes, pinched claws and similar difficulties.

The screened cage should be large enough to accommodate this litter box and an occasional swimming pool and a food dish and a watering can, without obligating the animal to run the gantlet when it is going elsewhere.

Another point to remember is that a ferret is a nosy, inquisitive, probing, pushing, searching animal. When it is awake it is constantly "ferreting" out openings, cracks and holes; if it cannot find any, it might just create a few. Provide simple housing, strongly built with a minimum of nooks and crannies for hidden or forgotten treasure. Hidden treasure is a partly eaten ear of cooked corn or a clamshell with a little meat still sticking to it or a bone with most of the meat gnawed off. These things tend to attract vermin and generate smells of their own. Don't deprive your pet of these treats; just move all these leftovers after a few hours.

Your pet will really suffer in really hot weather. A drip bottle will help it keep alive by providing a constant supply of fresh water, but this is only the bare minimum. You will have a healthier, happier pet if you *offer* a cool bath on a hot summer day. Don't grab your pet and toss it into your bathtub, but with very little intelligent and thoughtful effort you can encourage your pet to bathe and even swim in his own tub, on his own

The two-apartment cage may be entered from the screen end or the nestbox end without disturbing the other apartment. The water can is suspended by a wire. Your ferret will enjoy batting it around.

terms. The ferret will have a ball, and the total effect is one of great hilarity.

Try a basin of perhaps four to six inches deep and as large as will conveniently fit on a readily drained cage floor. There will be a good deal of splashing. You can be sure of that. Fill the basin with cool tapwater to within an inch of the top and toss in a ping pong ball or its equivalent. Your ferret will probably be in the water of his own volition within minutes.

On a hot summer day your pet will not only get some cooling comfort but will end up cleaner, and any smells will be reduced or eliminated. You need not dry your ferret with a towel unless you want to; so long as the weather is warm, he will dry out without taking a chill. Remember, there will be much splashing; plan to find about half the water you put in the basin elsewhere before the fun is over. Additionally, you may want or need to really wash your pet with a shampoo. Choose a mild brand that you would use on yourself, or better still one recommended for cats.

Your ferret will try to dig a tunnel in the water—let him. Your ferret will jump, dive, swim, walk under water, splash and do battle with the basin—let him. After five or ten minutes remove the basin and be sure there is some dry hay or clean absorbent rags for the little fellow to roll in and dry off. It might be a wise precaution for you to remove his litter tray during these proceedings.

When your pet remembers his heritage he is likely to pick up solid food and drag it to a corner or into the nest box before eating it. This may be something he learned as a kit with five hungry siblings ready to steal his tidbit. If you furnish large lumps of solid food and have more than one ferret in a cage this will surely happen. Then some of the food will be smeared in the cage corner and again you will end up with insects or decomposition. There are several things you can do about that. Offer only soft food which cannot be carried. Of course this spoils half the ferret's fun, but it also cuts *your* work nearly in half. Another alternative is to clean the cage promptly after meals. An outside cage can easily be hosed down from time to time. Just put your pet in a travel box for a few minutes and give the entire screened area a good swish and perhaps a pass or two with a scrubbing brush once every week or two. Try a little ammonia in the corners where the "accidents" happen.

A fine travel box is the one your pet dealer offers for use with cats. It is well ventilated, dark inside and

A cat traveling case makes a fine transporter for ferrets. Three ferrets can fit easily into a box intended for a large cat or a small dog. Don't neglect cool fresh drinking water, especially in summer. Wood chips make a good absorbent cage-floor covering.

amply large for one or two ferrets. Most people in the travel business don't really care to know about the taxonomic differences between ferrets and cats. Interestingly, *cats* are permitted in travel boxes on trains, buses and airplanes.

Fleas and ticks are controlled as you would for a cat. You pay your money and you take your choice from among the many products available.

Provide clean bedding, remove soiled litter, remove uneaten food and don't crowd your pets. Don't keep a ferret (or any other pet) unless you are willing to give it the opportunity to keep itself clean and healthy.

Activities

Aside from the basic functions of eating, sleeping, reproducing, etc., the ferret is famous for the active probing that his name has come to represent both as a common noun and a common verb in our language. As a pet, only the weasels come close, and among them only the rare and expensive otter makes a good pet. So, if you want full enjoyment for and from this kind of amusing companion, give him toys. A ball—ping pong to baseball size—is a good starter. The next is a tube, a tunnel, a conduit, a rathole. For the ferret who has "everything," give it a rathole and you have given it heaven-on-earth.

If you cannot afford a rathole, settle for some cardboard or plastic tubing three or four inches in diameter. Bends are great. "Y" and "T" joints are also great. The more complicated the route, the happier your pet will be. Two ferrets and twenty feet of four-inch jointed pipe are more fun than a large barrel of monkeys.

Small toys should be pushable or rollable, but not edible. Sponge rubber cannot be digested, and toys which might be torn apart should not be offered. The only type of dog chew product that is suitable is the Nylabone® , a flavor-impregnated artificial bone that is designed not to splinter but to wear down gradually. Nylabones are available at petshops. A *large* raw beef bone is a great toy, and what gets chewed off is good nourishment. Use your imagination; your pet will surely use his—all the time.

This paragraph could also appear under cages or cleanliness, since it ties all three together. Your ferret will be uncomfortable on a hot summer day. He sweats on his damp nose, but not much elsewhere, so keeping cool is a problem. If his nestbox is full of clean dry bedding and his screened cage is ready for a hosing anyway, you might try a wash-down without first locking him out of it. The results are apt to surprise you. Your pet will deliberately run through the stream, bite at it, and otherwise frolic in it like any eight-year-old child in front of an opened fire hydrant on a hot summer day. He will treat the cool spray as a toy, and the frolic will be good enough for home movies. You should carefully choose the time so that when, after five minutes of soaking, you shut the water off, your pet can dry off promptly and thoroughly in his bedding or in your towel.

Diet

Ferrets kill and eat rodents, moles, birds, beetles, grasshoppers, crickets, grubs and worms. They also eat berries, fruit, vegetables, milk, cereals, bread, cake, fish, eggs, table scraps and greaves. You don't know what greaves are? Well, that's all right; your pet will survive without greaves. But if you do have a source of really good greaves, you should put them in a feeding pan and pour boiling water over them and work up the mixture to a consistency of paste which should be fed warm. In some parts of the U.S., greaves are better known as cracklings.

There is some difference of opinion about milk in the diet of ferrets. Some say it causes severe diarrhea, and other pet keepers regularly provide it to females and their young on demand. Probably the best course for a beginner is to start cautiously. There is no question that ferrets enjoy drinking milk. How you feed it is for you to work out. You might want to dilute it with water, or feed only evaporated milk, or limit the quantity. Your pet surely should not end up with a high milk input, but rather should get a little milk regularly as a supplement and a treat. A box with an overhead hinged inward-swinging door and furnished with a dish of milk and a little nesting material inside might be a very useful device if your pet wanders out of his cage. For insurance, you might train your ferret to go into such a box for his milk against the time he gets loose outside.

In 1897, Nicholas Everitt told us that "when not at work, bread and milk form their staple diet," and that sometimes oatmeal is substituted for the bread. Jills with brood were given fresh meat and part of a cat's carcass was sometimes provided instead of the usual rats, birds, fowls and "ducks necks and such like."

Today the mink ranchers have made a more scientific study of our pet and his needs. In Denmark, the mink farmers are somehow associated with the herring fishermen, and the diet of the Danish ranch mink is relatively high in fish heads and entrails, but grain and milk supplements make up at least ⅓ of the total ration. In the U.S.A. and Canada the recommended diet averages out to 32% animal protein and 20% animal fat; the remainder is vegetable and cereal carbohydrate with some indigestible fiber.

Dry kibbled cat food supplemented by table scraps and milk makes a wholesome and balanced diet. If you keep several ferrets and live near a mink ranch, you may want to purchase their freshly prepared mix and freeze it in small portions for future use.

You should avoid candies and "junk foods" and whole, unmilled grains. Whole, uncooked corn kernels, for example, are virtually undigested in the short time they take to pass through a ferret, but a little boiled corn *meal* or corn *bread* wet with milk is a welcome treat for your pet.

Your ferret should always have fresh clean water available to drink, and two meals every day of solid food. He will not gorge himself on a routinely fed diet—give him all he will consume twice a day and a treat when you have him out of his cage for play. Females about to give birth and when lactating, and young ferrets being weaned, do well with extra milk *supplementing* their meals, but solid animal protein, fat, fiber, cereals and some fruit or vegetable should be included in every meal. If your pet gets a little milk daily, it is not as likely to suffer from milk-induced diarrhea as it might if it never had any previously.

If you feed your pet scraps from the table, you should try to provide, on the average, *not more than* two-thirds, and preferably not more than one-half, of the total weight of his intake from vegetable or cereal sources; the remainder might well be raw ground hamburger. Supplement this mix with a little milk and your pet will thrive. Feed the same animal on *just* dry dog kibbles or *just* canned fish for cats and you will certainly shorten its life.

Offer your pet a chicken bone or a beef bone to gnaw on from time to time. If you trap mice or find a fresh road-killed squirrel, you might offer them too.

The only problem with feeding your domestic ferret on whole wild fresh-killed birds and mammals is that you may also introduce parasitic worms, ticks and fleas. Storage in a freezer for a few days and then thawing before feeding will reduce this hazard considerably, but not completely.

You may discover that your pet enjoys raw or stewed fruits and vegetables like peaches, bananas, pears, lettuce, cucumber or sweet pepper. This is perfectly all right so long as the total input (within a few days) averages out to at least one-third animal meat, fat and organs, by weight.

If you find that your pet carries food to hiding places where it accumulates and spoils, consider the following:

1. It is competing with others for food.
2. It is about to give birth and is accumulating a larder.
3. You are overfeeding it.
4. It is nervous because of some animal or person.

If you wish to discourage this behavior, you might:
1. Remove the irritant.
2. Feed softer foods which cannot be carried.

You might, for example, add water to the canned dog or canned cat food and blend it in with a fork to the consistency of cooked cereal. Then the animal will be unable to carry away any pieces for hiding. Evaporated milk may be poured over stale bread which has been broken up into little bits to create the same effect. Fruits may be pureed to the texture of baby food. Of course, if you do all this an occasional "gnawing bone" will become a special treat and should be offered from time to time.

Health Care

Your ferret will shed some hair twice a year—this is normal. A new coat is frequently a dramatic color change from the previous. You need not ever comb, brush or clip your ferret's fur. Females expecting to whelp will sometimes pluck their hair to line the nest; this, too, is normal.

If your pet's ears trouble him, you might clean them with a little cotton–tipped stick—the same as you use on yourself. Your veterinarian may suggest an oil or antiseptic on the cotton.

As the ferret's nails grow, you can clip them with the same tool you use on your own nails or, better still, use the type made for cats and available from your pet shop. Be careful not to cut too close to the colored (living) part of his nails. Leave one-sixteenth of an inch of nail beyond the limit of the blood in each nail to avoid injury to your pet.

Diarrhea is usually the result of a dirty cage, stale food or too much milk.

Nail clipping, even with a gentle tame pet, deserves gloves, if only as a precaution. Cut only the part of the nail where no pink shows.

When you purchase your ferret you should get a document which shows where it came from on a U.S. Department of Agriculture Health Inspection Service Form.

If it has been inoculated for distemper or rabies this fact also should be documented.

Canine distemper, rabies, parasites, worms and other animal diseases are properly problems for your veterinarian, and he should be consulted. Feline distemper is rare in ferrets. Since the vaccines required for ferrets are not the same as those usually stocked by animal doctors for dogs and cats, you should make an appointment with your "vet" before you bring your pet in for his "shots."

You may decide to have your adult hob castrated as a dog is castrated or your jill altered as a cat is altered, and again your veterinarian can handle this chore. Anal glands on the male are sometimes removed surgically, but most pet keepers consider it unnecessary.

The disease of neglect in ferrets is foot rot; the feet swell and the skin cracks. This is a result of cold wet cages or dirty wet cages. A case of sore, split feet in your pet is no one's fault but yours. You must provide your pet with a clean, warm, dry nestbox so that he is not forced to constantly stand on wire mesh or cold damp soiled surfaces. You can cure foot rot with sanitation and antibiotic creams. Antibiotics alone will not correct the problem.

The common cold is also a problem with chilled or rundown specimens. Ferrets are prone to catch cold and quick to recover if their diet and housing are adequate.

Rabies vaccine *must* be of the type known as "inactivated." Young ferrets *must* be at least six months old before they are given a rabies vaccination. This is critical, since younger specimens may die or actually contract rabies from the wrong vaccine or inoculation at less than six months of age. One reference for your veterinarian to check is in the *Journal of Public Health*, Vol. 60, No. 6, June 1970.

Reproduction

Ferrets are born in spring or summer and are sexually mature the following spring; seven to eleven months is a good figure to work with. From then until they die of old age, they are capable of reproducing themselves.

When males are feeling sexy, they are very much so. A male will grab the female by the neck, and one fears that he is about to strangle her. When they mate, ferrets frequently take longer than you might expect if your experience has been with chickens or hamsters. Sometimes a mating pair will remain together for several hours. Don't disturb them, and nature will properly take its course.

The sex organs of ferrets don't show much except when they are ready to mate (in heat), and then the female's vulva will be swollen and colored pink. The male (hob) will hardly look like a male until the early spring, and then his testes will swell and become prominent.

After your pair has mated, the female's vulva should return to its normal appearance within a day or two. If it remains pink and swollen, for say three days, the mating was not successful, and the pair should be remated. Of course, if you keep the pair together, they will do it themselves with no help from you.

A mated (pregnant) jill may be kept with the hob until she begins to show nervousness or begins to make a nest. Sometimes in early spring she may pluck some of her fur to line the nest of soft hay which you should provide. When the time comes to separate hob from jill, try to work things out so that it is the hob that gets moved. She should not be subjected to *any* excitement before, during or immediately after the kits arrive.

The approximate time of gestation is 42 days, but sometimes several days will elapse between mating and implantation of the fertilized ova in the womb.

The pen for the jill should include a private, dark, secure, secluded area for her to bring forth her family. If you get nosey before they are at least two weeks old, you may cause her to kill or desert her babies. When the youngsters are about a month old, the hob may be returned to the pen, but he really isn't necessary. If you want a second litter that same summer, you may be able to re-mate the jill about two weeks after she stops nursing her litter.

The precise time of year when a ferret is ready to breed depends on the length of daylight and the temperature. Pets kept in the house frequently come into heat sooner than those kept outside.

The litter will be naked and blind at birth. They are about as large as a baby hamster when born, but grow rapidly. The female has seven workable teats for nursing her young and she will rarely have more than seven in her litter.

She will need a lot of food to produce the milk for a litter of six or so and this is your job. She will not overeat, so you can offer as much as she will consume, but you should remove uneaten food before it spoils. If she is accustomed to fresh or evaporated cow's milk, this is a good time to increase the ration of it. Just don't wait until after the litter is whelped and then push the milk—the shock to her digestive system will surely cause diarrhea and do more harm than good.

The natural breeding cycle of domestic ferrets in the Northern Hemisphere is March through August, and in the Southern Hemisphere it is September through February. Daylight is the governing factor, and the magic number is about sixteen hours. With sixteen hours of light, a male ferret will be ready and willing or even anxious to do his duty and a mature female will ovulate all year long! The long period of daylight is important for the female not only to induce ovulation but also to induce the production of milk (lactation). Of course, without the milk the litter would starve.

If your jill has been handled a lot before her confinement, she will be more tolerant of human interference after she whelps. She will nevertheless manage perfectly with no help from you. If she cannot, then the only alternative is professional veterinary help, which has to be expensive, and there is still no assurance that the delivery will be successful. So, in general, leave the jill strictly alone during her labor and *then*, after things settle down, you might want to sneak a quick look. Remove any that are stillborn and check for tangles. If the hay is long and the umbilical cords are also long, there may be a tangle of one or two kits in the hay, and this can be fatal to them.

At birth the kits weigh about five grams (one sixth of an ounce) each. From tip of nose to tip of tail, a newborn kit will measure just about three inches, of which the tail takes up between five-eighths and three-quarters of an inch. Two days later they will weigh seven grams and will measure nearly four inches. This phenomenal growth rate will continue for about a month.

Newborn ferrets look about the same regardless of whether they are brown, albino or any other color. The scant hair on their pink bodies is grey for dark varieties and white for albinos, but the only clear suggestion of future color is perhaps a tiny dot of pigment on the hairless nose. They grow rapidly; in three weeks their color will be evident and their eyes will be opening up.

Ferrets also mature rapidly. A four-month-old specimen looks for all the world like a four-year-old specimen.

The control of breeding cycles through light is nothing new to animal breeders; people have had lights in hen houses for years. One simple method of extending daylight for a caged ferret is with an incandescent light or a fluorescent lamp which goes on before dusk and remains on until sixteen hours after sunrise. You don't need glaring bright light; if you can read a newspaper it is bright enough. There are many clock-timers available to do this automatically and if you must have baby ferrets in Alfred, New York or Milton, Wisconsin or Salem, West Virginia in December, get that light going to add daylight hours.

Life Cycle in Quick Review

Ferrets born the previous spring and summer will be ready to breed in the following spring.

Jills will develop swollen and pink vulva when in heat, and hobs will develop swollen testes.

Mating will take ten minutes to several hours.

Jill's vulva will return to normal appearance in a week if she is pregnant. If not, she may be remated.

Jill will whelp 42 days after impregnation.

Jill may build nest and line it with some of her own fur about ten days before whelping. Male should be removed.

First litters average six or seven kits. Second litter of season is frequently smaller. Total kits per year are ten or eleven.

Newborn kits weigh five grams and grow rapidly. Kits' eyes open in four weeks. Hob may then rejoin his family.

Kits are weaned at six to eight weeks of age. Jill may come into heat when kits are weaned and may then be bred again.

Breeding requires 16 hours of light per day.

Life expectancy is nearly ten years.

By Comparison

Modern ferret fanciers are pioneers to the vast majority of people, especially young city people, who hardly know what a ferret is. If we list the facts about a few better-known mustelids, it might be easier to describe our pet to someone who knows nothing about it. It should be noted that for each of the animals chosen for comparison with the domestic ferret there are several species, subspecies and/or races, and these obviously are not all alike.

	Ferret	Weasel	Mink	Otter	Skunk
Wt. (max. lbs.)					
Male	5	one-sixth to ¾	3½	25	14
female	3	one-eighth to ½	1¾	10	10
Overall length (in.)					
Male	24	20	30	54	30
Female	18	12	20	much smaller	slightly smaller
Gestation (days)	42	220-337*	45+	60	60
Odor (scale of 5)	2	3	5	1	4
Fur Value (scale of 5)	2	1	4	5	3
Lifespan (years)	8-10	5	10	15	10
Domesticity (scale of 5)	5	1	2	4	3
Genus	*Mustela*	*Mustela*	*Mustela*	*Lutra*	*Mephitis*

*It may be that gestation in the weasel is not 220 to 337 days, but rather that after mating the sperm is stored in the body of the female and implanted in her womb long after copulation. This phenomenon is known as delayed implantation. Perhaps gestation (technically speaking, the growth and development of the embryo) takes only a month or so.

Man and Mustelidae

The family Mustelidae, "the seekers of mice," includes the stoat, ferret, weasel, ermine, mink, otter, fisher, marten, sable, European polecat, sea otter, badger, wolverine and skunks. There is some difference of opinion about the derivation of the word *Mustelidae*. A "seeker of mice" or "those who carry off mice" is probably as close as we can come, but some authors suggest that the name is derived from the animals' sometimes musty odor.

As everyone knows, the skunk will discharge the aromatic product of his anal glands upon provocation, and the wolverine will use his to mark off the boundaries of his real estate or the storage place of his uneaten food.

This trait of discharging distinctive odors is probably true of all members of the family to some extent. Ferrets are not especially smelly (and even these relatively inoffensive glands may be removed surgically by a veterinarian if necessary), but as a matter of fact, about 10,000 ferrets are currently raised and sold to pet keepers each year, and the number that have had or will have their anal glands removed is probably less than one per cent. Incidentally, the male ferret is mustier than the female.

The adults recognize each other and perhaps are sexually attracted by these scents. Each species has a distinctive odor, and while taxonomists recognize species by their teeth and other bone structures, it is important for members of a species to be recognizable to each other.

There is some evidence that a rodent recognizes the presence of a ferret by this odor even in the blackness of his tunnel and will try to escape without ever seeing his mortal enemy.

For pet keepers, the slightly musty odor of a ferret can be controlled without too much effort. Clean cages help. Fresh bedding helps. Occasional bathing helps. Some vegetable foods are reported to help. Relief from stress certainly helps; a relaxed ferret will release less anal gland fluid. As mentioned previously, some pet-keepers will have their veterinarian remove the anal glands and also castrate a male pet. This is a perfectly appropriate option, especially for male specimens kept in the home. Females are sometimes altered surgically to reduce their sex urge, but it is not usually considered worth bothering to remove their anal glands, since their mustiness is so mild anyway.

The family Mustelidae includes a number of animals that have high-quality fur. One has only to quietly drop words like ermine, mink, fisher, marten, otter, sea otter and sable, and deaf ladies' eyes light up. The sea otter is probably the world's most valuable fur. On a square inch basis it beats even the fabled chinchilla, hands down. Sea otter pelts have sold at wholesale fur auctions for over one thousand dollars each.

Ranch-raised mink have become a big industry in Denmark, Canada and the northern states in the U.S.A. One modestly sized mink ranch in the U.S. currently uses over one ton of mink food daily! In 1960 the world production of ranch mink for the fur trade was 8,500,000 pelts, and by 1970 it had risen to 25,000,000. At an average of $40 per pelt, this works out to $1,000,000,000 per year, yes, one billion dollars—and going up. By comparison, during 1970 only 430,000 wild minks were trapped and sold in the fur trade. Some mink farms also produce a few ferrets for the fur industry. A ferret pelt is sold under the name "fitch"; it is less desirable and less expensive than mink, but since the productivity of ferrets is higher than that of mink, some ranchers can make a little money in that market too. When kept on a ranch, ferrets and mink are caged and fed in generally the same manner.

In addition to ferrets, other mustelids such as otters, badgers, skunks and mink have been kept as housepets. Of these four, the otter is the most desirable. Otters are easily tamed, especially if started when young, and they are acknowledged as intelligent, amusing, clean and long-lived. Duck hunters have even trained otters to retrieve downed ducks, and fishermen have sent pet otters into the water after fish.

One difficulty with the keeping of otters, badgers, skunks and mink is that these species are considered wild furbearers in the eyes of the law, and owners in many places are regulated accordingly.

Not so much so with the domesticated ferret. In Connecticut, for example, one may not hunt rabbits with a ferret, but a license to possess one pet ferret may be purchased from any town clerk for a dollar, and to keep any number over one, a fee of five dollars is charged. With this license, in Connecticut, you may legally possess ferrets. The distinction between the ferret and the other mustelids seems to be that the ferret has been with man for so long that he can hardly survive in most places without man. When a young person approaches his parents with a list of reasons why he should be permitted to keep ferrets, he might mention that one.

European superstition has it that a case of whooping cough can be cured by administration of a drink of milk which was "blessed" by a ferret. In case you are not familiar with the ferret's method of blessing milk, he simply laps up a few tonguefuls from a dish—what remains is thereby blessed. Some Irish health-food experts consider milk so blessed to be "the one real remedy you can put your entire faith in."

In addition to pet, rat control and fur pelt aspects of ferrets in man's eco-system, it should be mentioned that these animals have been kept in laboratories for many years for research and disease prevention.

They are small and long-lived and are subject to some of the same diseases that attack cats, dogs and people. This makes them ideal for generating vaccines. Your dog or cat likely received a distemper or rabies inoculation which derived from a ferret.

Your pet ferret is vulnerable to the common cold. He sniffles and sneezes much as you do, and since he is easier to control and observe, many medical studies about colds are performed on ferrets.

Considering the demands for these animals, one might well wonder whether this pet ferret of yours might be a stepping-stone to fame and fortune. Forget it, unless you are already established as a successful ranch breeder of mink.

The know-how, captial investment, sources of food and contacts in the marketplace are well established for ferrets in the same way as in the ranch-mink industry, and logically this is where it belongs. A vaccine manufacturer or a research laboratory wants an assured supply of genetically pure, healthy animals, all within a particular age group. No home-hobby-retirement-investment-pet keepers can possibly compete.

Bear in mind that the breeder's price for ferrets is *less* than one half of what you paid for your pet, and at that they are making a profit. Simple arithmetic will show you that it is impossible for a home breeder to make money at these prices.

What you can do, and do successfully, is to keep and enjoy a pet, or perhaps a breeding pair. With a pair you might produce an average of eight kits a year for your friends and local pet shops. It is amazing how fast you can saturate the ferret market in your town with one or two bred females. If you must ship your animals to dispose of them, you will encounter packaging problems, inoculation problems, U.S. Department of Agriculture regulations, airline rules and state laws restricting importation to certain places.

The potential for profit in ferret pelts (fitch) has been fully explored and exploited by mink farmers. You can rest assured that if there were a dollar to be found, they would long since have found it.

For those who never say die, yes, there is hope. New color varieties are always in demand for pelts and pets, and they command a premium in the marketplace. If you want to breed ferrets with this in mind, you should schedule at least ten profitless years of carefully planned matings of selected specimens. Even without any dramatic mutant forms to start, you should, with one hundred breeders and a professionally guided genetic plan to work from, be able to establish a new color or marking pattern which breeds true. Ideally, it will be sex-linked in a way that gives you continued control. For example, you may have a strain of males which, when mated to females of another, always produces young of a particular color or color pattern. However, to keep control, these specially colored young should not produce their own color when mated to each other. Impossible? No! There are strains of poultry where this is done on a routine basis for egg or meat production, and "sex-linked" eggs or chickens can be purchased from specialists in poultry all over the world. Of course, a chicken has more universal appeal than a ferret, but the same principles of genetics are applicable.

One cautionary remark is in order here. Hire a lawyer to check your game laws, zoning laws, restrictive covenants, easements and local regulations before ordering all those cages.

Another cautionary remark is also in order. You JUST LEARNED about ferrets and you are excited about their various traits and potentials, but you should remember that ferrets have been with us for more than 2,000 years as *domestic animals*. This compares with 10,000 years for the dog and 5,000 for the cat. The ferret has already been thoroughly exploited; now it's your turn to relax and enjoy your pet simply as a pet. It is surely tempting to build castles in the air, but your chances of finding fame or fortune would be better selling magazine subscriptions or taxidermy lessons by telephone.

Hunting with Ferrets

We can assume that after ferrets were first domesticated 2,000 or so years ago, they remained within our culture primarily for the purpose of hunting with them. They are not desirable as human food, their fur was readily available from wild specimens and their value as pets at that time is not recorded. However, the record is clear that by the first century after Christ, ferreting was practiced in Africa, Asia and Europe. The Greek geographer Strabo (B.C. 63 to A.D. 21), tells us that the ferret was introduced to Spain from Africa, and the Roman naturalist Pliny (23 to 79 A.D.) mentions the sport of hunting rabbits with ferrets.

By the time of Queen Victoria, the British patent office was inundated with designs of ferret cages; in the U.S.A., after the first World War, the Department of Agriculture was publishing bulletins on these animals, primarily for rodent control.

It is possible that the genetic origin of the ferret is confused because of the considerable length of time it has been domesticated and the geographic area which is involved. There is some speculation that the unstable colors and the variable size of ferrets are the results of crosses between Asiatic and European polecats over the course of years. For the record, it should be made absolutely clear that the native American blackfooted ferret is in no way involved in the genetic make-up of our domestic animal.

Hunting rabbits with ferrets in the U.S. is not legal, but killing rats is a licensed activity in many places, and even today some exterminators successfully use ferrets on rodents. Usually, when ferrets are used to hunt rats, they are let down a rathole; if the hole is a dead end, the ferret kills the rat in his nest. If the rat's nest has another opening, it will surely try to escape, and then a small terrier is employed to kill the escaping rodent. Both the dog and the ferret seem to take naturally to this work without too much training. When all the rats are driven out of their tunnels, the ferret will surface and is then taken in hand by his owner. If the ferret corners a rat, he will surely kill it, drink its blood and eat some parts. When the ferret is sated, it will sleep for eight or nine hours and the hunter can go off and play cribbage or a round of golf, because his ferret is not about to stir.

When the little hunter does wake up, hungry again, he may be lured from the rathole with a little milk or some other treat.

When rabbit hunting was legal, the ferret was either muzzled or "coped" with a loop of string through his lips and around his head to prevent him from killing and eating his prey. The rabbit would leave home through the back door and the hunter would shoot if he spied long ears. Fortunately for ferrets, *their* ears are always short.

Ferrets for ratting are necessarily small—no larger in diameter than rats is the ideal size. Today, the pet ferret is selectively bred larger, and adult males that weigh as much as a small cat are not uncommon.

Color

For centuries the classic color of a ferret was white or yellowish-white. Its eyes were pink. It was an albino. Mated, white ferrets produced white offspring, because in ferrets albinism is a simple recessive trait.

Today, dark-eyed ferrets in other colors are also available. Some breed true and some don't. The brown ferret is also known as sable. The coarse guard hairs are dark brown and the softer undercoat is creamy yellow. The legs and most of the tail are dark brown. The muzzle and area between eyes and ears is pale; a dark mask surrounds the eyes and crosses the bridge between them. This is the dominant "natural" color trait, and the colors resemble those of the European polecat.

The Siamese is a recessive mutation which resembles a Siamese cat with its dark markings at the extremities. Older specimens are more strongly marked. This color trait is recessive to sable.

White-footed and white-throated "sables" are also common. Sometimes they are called silver mitt.

Silver is a new color variety which has many white guard hairs instead of brown; in silvers, the undercoat tends to be more white than yellow.

There is no apparent linkage between color and any other trait. Sables are no more intelligent than albinos or Siamese. The bright-light vision of an albino may be impaired by the lack of pigment in his pink eyes, but albino hunting ferrets have been with us for over twenty centuries and, although crosses with wild dark-eyed dominants have always been available, the albino has always been the most desired color form.

Genetically pure sable strains (**BB**) are probably possible to achieve, but unless someone is willing to establish such a strain and keep track of the pedigrees— a time-consuming and expensive effort—we cannot be sure that our brown sable pet, when mated to another brown-sable, will produce a litter of brown-sables.

If we had a pair of brown-sables both of which have a recessive trait (**Bb**) for albino, it is possible that they might produce some white offspring. Statistically, it works out like this:

B is the dominant brown genetic trait; one **B** is sufficient to produce brown color.

b is the recessive albino trait. Since it is recessive, it takes two **b**'s to bring out albinism. (There is also a possibility that there is more than one strain of albino ferret and that their color chromosomes are not arranged identically. That would complicate the issue beyond the scope of this book.)

An albino would have in its genetic make-up **bb**.

A sable, if pure, would be **BB**.

A sable might actually have a hidden recessive **b**, and then would be **Bb**.

Assume no new mutations for these diagrams; then two pure dominant **BB** sables mate and the offspring will be all pure **BB** dominant sable:

	B	B
B	BB	BB
B	BB	BB

Expected ratios of offspring resulting from mating of two sable ferrets not carrying recessives for any other color: 100% pure brown sables (**BB**).

If two albinos (**bb**) mate, their offspring will all be **bb** pure recessive albino.

	b	b
b	bb	bb
b	bb	bb

Expected ratios of offspring resulting from mating of two pure albino ferrets: 100% pure albinos (**bb**).

If an albino (**bb**) were mated to a pure dominant brown-sable **BB**, all the young would be brown sable to look at, but each would have a recessive genetic trait for albino.

Expected ratios of offspring resulting from mating of a pure albino ferret to a pure sable ferret: 100% sables that carry the recessive gene for albinism (**Bb**).		**B**	**B**
	b	**Bb**	**Bb**
	b	**Bb**	**Bb**

If an albino **bb** were mated to a brown-sable with a recessive for albino (**Bb**), there would be a statistical possibility for both colors.

Expected ratios of offspring resulting from mating of a pure albino ferret to a sable ferret carrying the recessive gene for albinism: 50% sable that carry the recessive gene for albinism (**Bb**), 50% pure albinos (**bb**).		**B**	**b**
	b	**Bb**	**bb**
	b	**Bb**	**bb**

Fifty percent of the offspring (over the long haul) will be **bb** albino, and fifty percent will be brown-sable with the recessive trait for albino hidden in their genes.

And finally, if two brown-sables each with the recessive albino genetic trait were mated, the long-haul statistical output would be:

Expected ratios of offspring resulting from mating of two sable ferrets that each carry the recessive gene for albinism: 25% pure sables (**BB**); 50% sables carrying the recessive gene for albinism (**Bb**); 25% pure albinos (**bb**).		**B**	**b**
	B	**BB**	**Bb**
	b	**Bb**	**bb**

Index